A Study in Wisdom, 2nd edition
Copyright© 2014 by Learning for Life Press

Web site: http://www.learningforlifepress.com
Email: info@learningforlifepress.com
The address for Learning for Life Press is:
162 MorningStar Road
Venice, FL 34285

Sign up for Dr. Simpson's free e-newsletter with practical help on relationships, parenting, and living. Register for free and download free articles that are immediately useful for family life. Website: http://www.learningforlifepress.com

All rights reserved. No portion of this book may be reproduced in any form without written permission from Learning for Life Press and the author except by a reviewer, who may quote brief passages in a review. You have permission to photocopy pages 15, 16, all coloring pages with each lesson, Bible Chart, Owl Cards, and Stick Puppets for your family's use.

Special thanks to Joanna Jarc Robinson, Ph.D for her artwork, editing help, and ideas throughout this book. Find her at: http://jart1473.wix.com/joannarobinson.

Printed in the United States of America.
ISBN 978-0-9988624-5-3

Preface

I would like to thank my children Lane, Daniel, Quen, Anne, and Michael. Knowing you and being a part of your lives enriches me more than I can say. While none of us has lived a completely wise life, teaching you this study made me confront my own choices and challenged me to seek a life of wisdom as well. May we grow through being teachable, courageous, humble, honest with ourselves, and honest with each other. I would like to acknowledge Susan Simpson for organizing my initial study. Thanks also to Michael Simpson for preproduction help.

Table of Contents

Introduction	Page 4
How to Use This Program	Page 5-7
Step One	Page 8-9
Step Two	Page 10-11
Step Three	Page 12
Step Four	Page 13
Step Five	Page 14
Treasure Chest	Page 15
Memory Bags	Page 16
Verses from Proverbs	Page 17
Lesson One: Knowing God	Page 18-19
Lesson Two: Helping Others	Page 20-21
Lesson Three: Loving Others	Page 22-23
Lesson Four: Choosing Self-Control	Page 24-25
Lesson Five: Staying Calm When Angry	Page 26-27
Lesson Six: Thinking Before Acting or Reacting	Page 28-29
Lesson Seven: Trusting God	Page 30-31
Lesson Eight: Avoiding Gossip	Page 32-33
Lesson Nine: Avoiding Bad Situations	Page 34-35
Lesson Ten: Making Good Choices	Page 36-37
Lesson Eleven: Choosing Good Behaviors	Page 38-40
Lesson Twelve: Following Rules	Page 41-42
Lesson Thirteen: Learning from Mistakes	Page 43-44
Lesson Fourteen: Staying Humble	Page 45-46
Lesson Fifteen: Learning from Others	Page 47-48
Lesson Sixteen: Admitting Wrong-Doing	Page 49-51
Lesson Seventeen: Avoiding Bullies	Page 52-53
Lesson Eighteen: Controlling Your Temper	Page 54-55
Lesson Nineteen: Correcting Mistakes	Page 56-58
Lesson Twenty: Choosing Wise Friends	Page 59-60
Lesson Twenty-One: Avoiding Foolish People	Page 61-62
Lesson Twenty-Two: Obeying God	Page 63-64
Lesson Twenty-Three: Trusting God's Word	Page 65-66
Lesson Twenty-Four: God Lights the Way	Page 67-68
Lesson Twenty-Five: Respecting God's Wisdom	Page 69-70
Review All Verses	Page 71
Right and Wrong, Morality, and Sin	Page 72-73
A Suggestion of How to Teach Children about Sin	Page 74
Through the Bible	Page 75-76
Bible Chart	Page 77
Wise Owl Cards	Page 78
Stick Puppets	Pages 79-81

Introduction

When my children were younger, I noticed their desire to learn about good and bad in the world. This was frequently illustrated by one of them asking me when watching a TV show, "Is he a bad guy or a good guy?" For young children, this curiosity emerges in the natural process of intellectual development as they try to understand concepts of good and bad, pleasure and pain, opposites on an anchor point of a concept or experience.

We learn by understanding the simple endpoints for a concept or idea - that is how we begin our knowledge of values - but the beginning is not the end. What we know about either/or constructs at the start eventually gives way to more complex learning. As it turns out, we cannot easily categorize people or life into two groups.

Since life is not always clear cut (good people sometimes act badly, and bad people sometimes act properly), I decided to teach my children to use the Book of Proverbs as a model for assessing human behavior, particularly in the area of good (wise) and bad (foolish) decisions. The Book of Proverbs is a concise wisdom book useful for this purpose; a book that has stood the test of time. My goals for this study are:

    To acquaint children with the wisdom literature
    To help children learn what wisdom looks like
    To encourage children to apply wisdom principles in daily life

I found that I reached these goals with my children through this study. After many months of work on the subject of wisdom, they began to analyze stories spontaneously to determine who was being "wise" and who was being "foolish." Seeing them internalize what they had learned was exciting. Listening to them think through the choices in an encounter was wonderful.

I sincerely hope this study helps you guide your children in such a way that they will honor wisdom in their lives more highly than intelligence, athleticism, beauty, and popularity. I hope that whatever career or field they pursue, your children will be able to express wisdom throughout their lives, and God's ways will guide your family. As James Truslow Adams stated, "There are two educations. One should teach us how to make a living, and the other - how to live." May your children live lives that are worth living.

How to Use this Program

The study of wisdom is an exciting one for children because it helps them deal more effectively with the world around them. This book will start your children on a study and a method of decision making that will last a lifetime.

You will find words for the parent to read to the child in **bold font** (or letters) and directions about the activity in *italicized* letters.
On page 15, you will find an image of a Treasure Chest and on page 16, images of four Memory Gold Bags. Please photocopy the treasure chest page as many times as you need to and use it with the Memory Gold Bags. Photocopy the Memory Gold Bags as much as you need to as well. As your child memorizes a verse, help him or her write that verse on a bag. Paste or tape each bag on the photocopied treasure chest page.

This study has three sections.
The first section is, "An Introduction to Wisdom" and it has five steps. In this section, your children will learn about why wisdom is important in daily life, and how to obtain it.
The second section, "Verses from Proverbs," introduces your children to several verses from the wisdom book, Proverbs, which readers can find in the Jewish Scriptures, or what Christians call "The Old Testament." This section also provides methods to help children

memorize the proverbs.

The third section is an application of the knowledge from sections one and two. Entitled, "Through the Bible," this section helps your children to gain insight and make real-life connections to Bible stories you read (or they read themselves), applying the truths of Proverbs to the stories. This inductive method of study establishes the thinking process that leads to wisdom.

For section three, I suggest you use a Bible storybook for children, which is appropriate for their age level. I recommend *The Read 'n Grow Picture Bible* (Hardcover: 322 pages, Publisher: Thomas Nelson, ISBN-10: 084991163X and ISBN-13: 978-0849911637). Another good resource is *The Children's Bible in 365 Stories* (Hardcover: 416 pages, Publisher: David C. Cook, ISBN-10: 0745930689 and ISBN-13: 978-0745930688.) I refer to these books in this study. *The Read 'n Grow Picture Bible* is currently out of print as of fall 2014; however, there are new and used copies available online through Amazon and eBay. Although there are a few stereotypic images within *The Read 'n Grow Picture Bible*, it was clearly my children's favorite and became the only one we used. If you cannot obtain a copy, please contact me.

I have paraphrased all the Bible verses for children. You may use any version of the verse you prefer for your family. For this reason, I have not printed the verses on the memory gold bags. Please write your version of the verse for your children to memorize.

Most learning requires repetitive exposure to the material or skill. This is true about wisdom learning as well. In Proverbs and the other wisdom, there is a repetitive or overlapping pattern of teaching. This Study of Wisdom is no exception. Your children will be learning similar principles as they go along. Don't be alarmed if it feels somewhat repetitive. Allow them to explore the many angles and applications of a truth through creative play and storytelling. *Use the stick puppets in* the appendix to further the learning, repeating lessons with all new examples, guided by your child's imagination.

In the appendix, you will also find Wise Owl cards. Cut them out along the dotted lines. When you observe your child showing a wise behavior or a wise choice, give your child one of the owl cards. See how many cards your child can collect in one week or one day. Verbally reinforce wise behaviors, too.

At the end of the book, you will find a series of character puppets. Allow your child to color them then cut them on the dotted lines. Glue each character to a craft stick. Encourage your child to use the puppets to practice Proverb wisdom! Have your child act out different scenarios or situations. What would the characters say and do? How do the characters feel? How would the characters solve their problem? What would God say to each character? Encourage your child to explore wise language and problem solving with the puppets.

Also, be sure to play the Think It, Feel It, Say It Board Game that builds on and helps children learn more about the content in this guide. Enhance your children's wisdom and maturity with this exciting game of decision, expression, thinking skills, and loads of laughter. Ages: 6 - Above   Players: 2 - 8 The game offers children a fun way to explore more about emotions, others, life, and making good choices. Play the game as a family and get to know each other in new ways.

An Introduction to Wisdom
STEP ONE

Parent: Today we are going to begin a study of wisdom. Wisdom is something that can help you throughout your life. It can be like a great friend. Someone who keeps wisdom close to the heart is a "wise" person. I want to be wise in my life and maybe you will want to be wise, too.

How would you describe wisdom? A dictionary is a book that explains what words mean. One dictionary explains wisdom this way: "Wisdom takes insights gleaned from the knowledge of God's way and applies them to the daily walk." (The New Bible Dictionary) Wow! That's a lot to understand.

An easier way to say that is:
"Wisdom is making good choices that follow God's ways."

Give me examples of choices you make every day (e.g., I choose which clothes to wear, I choose which book to read, I choose what to eat, and how to play). **How can choices lead to good or bad things?**

Let us look at the life of a man who lived thousands of years ago, and an important choice he made about his life.

> *Read the story of King Solomon receiving the throne, I Kings Chapter 2, Read 'n Grow Picture Bible, pp. 138-139, The Children's Bible, p. 148. The central point is the fact that God placed Solomon on David's throne as king. Discuss the importance of following God's commandments as the king.*

Possible questions:
Parent: What is the job of a king, like Solomon?
Would you like the job of being king?
Is the king's job a difficult one? Why or why not?
Whom does the king have to listen to, or please? (e.g., everyone in his kingdom, God)

Would it be hard for a king to follow God?
> (e.g., The king might feel as though he is more powerful than God. The king might feel like the rules are not for him. A king might feel like he has to please everyone; that he has huge responsibilities and huge potential for failure. A king may not know whom he can trust. A king may not have prior training on how to lead a nation.)

What would help a king to be a good king?
> (e.g., Good advisors, knowing God's way, making wise choices, a willingness to follow God)
> *Tell the story of Solomon's dream found in chapter 3:3-15, Read 'n Grow Picture Bible, pp. 140-141, The Children's Bible, p. 149. Emphasize Solomon's desire for wisdom, and the idea that wisdom comes from God.*

Possible questions:
What did Solomon desire the most? (to make good choices as king)
Why? (Solomon had to make many big decisions to lead the country, decisions he had never faced before. Many people wanted different things from him. He felt like people were pulling him in different directions.)

*Note to parents: This starts the awareness of being pulled in different directions, feeling conflicted, even tempted...which will occur in your child's life from time to time.

What did God give to Solomon? (wisdom)
Why do you think He did? (He knew Solomon needed God's way to guide him, just as we need it.)

STEP TWO

Parent: Solomon wanted wisdom more than anything. He wanted to make sure his daily choices as a king would be good ones. He made many wise decisions as the king and even helped write a book about wisdom.
(Show your children the Book of Proverbs in your Bible.)

In Chapter 8: Verse 19, King Solomon described wisdom as "better than gold, even better than the finest pure gold you could ever find."

Now, Solomon was a very rich king who had chests full of gold. What does this verse tell you about him at this time in his life? Why wouldn't he be satisfied with just his gold?

If wisdom is so important, how can someone get it? How did Solomon find wisdom?
Let's look at the first chapter of Proverbs, verse 7. Solomon tells us how he became wise and how we can become wise, too.

"How can a man become wise? The first step is to trust and respect the Lord." Let's talk about trusting God.
(Read Proverbs 3:1-8.)

Parent: Do we have any reasons to trust God? (e.g., I think I can trust God because He made us, and like a good parent, He knows what's best for us.)

For older children: **Sometimes it may be hard to trust God, especially when we can't see Him and when things don't go our way.**

What are the reasons to trust God?
   (e.g., His love, His power, His knowledge, He is the Creator)

Why should we trust God?
   (e.g., He made us, He loves us, and He knows what we need)

Activity: *To convey the idea of trust, you can have your child do a "trust fall" with you. Have your child stand perfectly straight, arms by his or her side, legs locked, and looking forward. You stand behind your child, ready to catch him or her securely. AT YOUR WORD, have your child fall straight back. If your child bends his or her legs or steps back, it will not work properly. Your child must totally trust you to catch him or her. Do not make jokes during this exercise. BE SURE to catch your child. At first, stand very close to your child where he or she can comfortably "let go". Gradually, let your child fall farther back before you catch him or her. Be careful not to go too far. One slip in catching your child and the trust will be hard to get back, and your child could get hurt. The purpose of this experience is to see and feel what trust really requires.*

Parent: **For you to trust that I will catch you when you fall back, you must believe two things about me:**
   1. **I am powerful enough to hold you up. You would never let a two-year-old child catch you, would you?**
   2. **I care enough about you not to let you fall for any reason.**

Do you believe those two things about me? Do you trust me?

Are these two things true about God? Is He powerful? Does He

care about you? I believe He does. How would it feel to fall into God's arms or trust God completely?

Do you feel a little scared or uncertain about trusting God, especially since we cannot see Him? Do you feel excited and hopeful about letting yourself go, the point where you completely trust God to guide you in your life.

STEP THREE

Many years ago, and sometimes even today, battles and wars happen...where people or armies fight each other. It is sad, but it is true. Here is a story about King David, King Solomon's father. As a young man, probably a teenager, before he was a king, David found himself in a fight with a giant warrior. This happened in 1000 BC, or about 3000 years ago.

Read the story of David and Goliath, Read 'n Grow Picture Bible, pp. 122-123, The Children's Bible, p.119.

Possible questions:
Why did David fight this battle?
Whom did David trust with his life?
How did David learn to trust God?

(He learned to trust God by taking care of his father's sheep. Previously, David relied upon God to help him fight a bear and a lion (1 Samuel 17:36). He fought off a lion and bear in Judea (they are extinct now). He became skilled with the slingshot. To this day, young men in the near east can use the slings effectively. David learned courage in the face of fear - a courage borne out of trusting God.)

How can we learn to trust God more fully?

(By knowing Him more and by trusting Him repeatedly, we get better at it.)

STEP FOUR

Review Step Two. **Would you like to be a wise person? How can you be one?**

> *Read the story of Noah and the ark, Read 'n Grow Picture Bible, pp. 16-19, The Children's Bible, p.7. The emphasis is on trusting/respecting God. Discuss Noah's "fear" of God.*

Possible questions:
This is a story of a great flood. Floods happen when large amounts of water rush across the land. A puddle or a lazy stream is not very dangerous, but a flood can cause great damage. In this story, Noah obeyed what God told him, which saved his life and protected his family.

Is God powerful? How do you know?
(He created heaven and Earth. He created people. He is wise...)

Why should we respect and trust God?
(He can protect us. He can lead us into good choices that make a happy life.)

Does God take care of His people?
(We must trust him to take care of his people...)

How can we learn to respect God more?
(e.g., By knowing Him more, reading the Bible, hearing how God works in other people's lives, etc.)

STEP FIVE

Let us talk about what we have learned about wisdom so far. How can we acquire wisdom? How can we become wise?

In order to trust and respect the Lord, we must know Him more fully. How can we do that? When can we make time to learn more about Him?
(e.g., By praying, going to church, helping others, by being still and thinking about God, reading the Bible, asking others what they know about God, looking for what He is doing in our lives.)

Let us now ask our Loving Creator to help us know Him better, to trust and respect Him more.

Pray with your child. Ask God to help guide your choices to be wise, and pray that you are able to learn from choices that are not wise; and that your children will learn from their choices, too.

Two points of emphasis in the wisdom study:

1. All good things come from God, even our good intentions and desires. We must seek Him in all things.
2. Both parent and child need wisdom to do what the Lord has called us to do, and we both receive that wisdom in the same manner – by honoring, respecting, and learning from the Lord. This is a path we walk together.

Wisdom is better than gold, even pure gold.

Memory Bags – Copy this page as needed. Cut out the bags. Write your own version of a verse on each bag. Encourage your child to memorize the verse. When he or she knows it well, glue the bag on the page with the treasure chest.

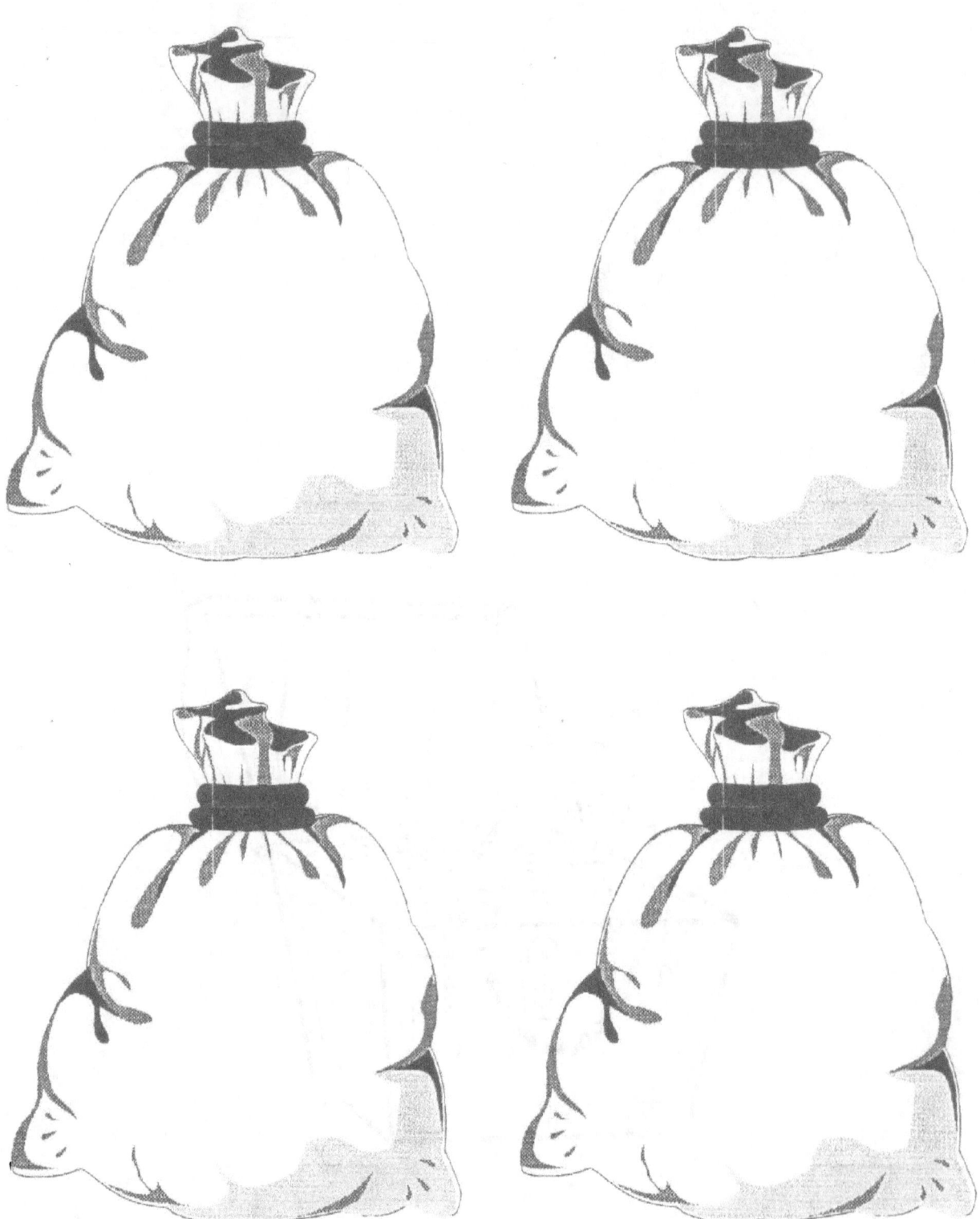

In the following lessons, you will introduce your child to verses that teach how a wise person behaves. You may want your child to memorize these verses, or you can review them on a regular basis to help your child remember about the qualities of a wise person.

If you choose to have your child memorize the verses, you may want to begin by putting the picture of the treasure chest (from page 14), on the wall. Photocopy the treasure chest page for each child in the family. Use the memory gold bags (page 15) to write the memory verses. Have your child put a new bag near the chest whenever he or she has memorized the verse.

As you teach your child about wisdom, be sure to explain that the opposite of wisdom is a bad choice (or if you prefer, foolishness). Proverbs repeatedly show the contrast between the wise person and the unwise person. You do not need to dwell upon this point, but mention it periodically. Everyone acts foolishly from time to time. Be sure that you do not label a child as a fool. The word "fool" in our culture may mean something about a person's worth. It can sound devaluing. This kind of shaming is unhealthy. Instead, focus on the misbehavior as an unwise behavior or choice. A child's misbehavior does not mean that he or she is inherently foolish. Be sure to respect your child's dignity and worth.

Each lesson contains a memory verse, a story, or an activity to help teach the verse, and an application for the verse. You may present one or two verses each week or as you like. Review the memory verses every day.

LESSON ONE
Knowing God is the beginning of a smart life.
Proverbs 9:10

  **The Jewel in the Verse:** God has the roadmap for life. In fact, He is the roadmap.

DISCUSSION AND ACTION: **Can you tell me one way we can know about God? Let us read a story that tells us about who God is and how He acts.**

There was another big battle thousands of years ago. Joshua was doing what God wanted him to do and it led to a big fight.
Read the story about Joshua's army and the Amorites, found in Joshua 10, Read 'n Grow Picture Bible p. 94-95, The Children's Bible p. 82.

What did we learn about God from this story?
Write the responses on the board or paper. (Possible answers: God has power over the sun, the earth, and space. God keeps His promises.)

Another way we learn about God is in our daily lives. This week, talk to family members about how God works in their daily lives. Look for Him in your life and tell us what you learn.

What is happening in the picture? Why is the grown-up reading? How could reading help the people in the picture?

This week, share what you learned about God with your family.
Color the picture.

The knowledge of God is the beginning of understanding.
Proverbs 9:10

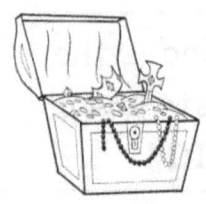
LESSON TWO
A wise person helps those in need.
Proverbs 29:7

  **The Jewel in the Verse:** Helping others is part of a well-lived life.

DISCUSSION AND ACTION:
Look at the coloring picture for this verse on the opposite page. Make up a story about the two characters you see.

Why is the little bear bringing the older bear a pie? Who do you think made the pie? What is the older bear feeling? What is the little bear feeling? Do you think there are people around us who might be lonely or sad? Do you think there are people we might see or know who could use our help?

A wise person helps those in need.
Proverbs 29:7

LESSON THREE

Good people not only love others, they love animals and take care of them. Mean people don't care what other people or animals feel, and they sometimes enjoy hurting others.

Proverbs 12:15

The Jewel in the Verse: Wise people care for other people, as well as for all of God's creatures.

DISCUSSION AND ACTION: This lesson is about empathy. It is about caring for everyone and everything along the line, down to the littlest of God's creatures.

If we have a pet, what should we be willing to do in order to be kind to that pet? If we meet somebody who seems to have problems, looks or acts differently from us, how should we act toward that person? If we notice someone is not taking care of an animal or child, how do we feel? What should we do?

Discuss how each child has feelings and that it is good to remember that others have feelings, too. We should remember that even animals have some feelings. Being kind is always the best choice.

Tell a story about the picture of the bear feeding the birds. What is the bear thinking? What are the birds thinking? What might the birds say to the bear? How might the birds be feeling? What is the bear feeling?

> Help take care of some animals this week. Feed the birds!
> Color the picture.

Good people not only love others, they love animals and take care of them. Mean people don't care what other people or animals feel, and they sometimes enjoy hurting others.
Proverbs 12:15

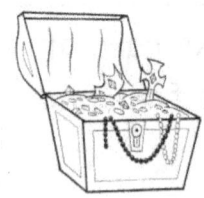

LESSON FOUR
Learning patience and self-control is a great thing, but people with a bad temper hurt others and show bad choices.
Proverbs 14:29

  **The Jewel in the Verse:** Self-control is the best way to live.

DISCUSSION AND ACTION: This lesson is about learning to control your feelings, especially anger. We have many different feelings to manage, including pleasant feelings like excitement, happiness, pride, and love. We have unpleasant feelings to manage such as sadness, envy, helplessness, fear, and anger. God says that wise people learn to control their feelings so that we can make right choices and avoid behaving badly.

> **How can we control strong feelings?**
> *(e.g., Pay attention to what you feel. Ask yourself, "What am I feeling right now?" or "What is a good thing to do with this feeling?" and then do your best to make a wise choice). Maybe tell someone you trust just what you feel. Teach your child not to ignore a feeling but to understand what it is and why it is there. Then you can have some control over it, rather than just reacting without thinking.*

Let's talk about the next picture. What feeling is the girl bear showing in each picture? Tell a short story about what might have made her feel each feeling. Tell about a time when you had each of those feelings, too. I think it is good to learn about your feelings, even the unpleasant ones, so you can control them better. What do you think?

Talk about each feeling. When have you felt that way?
Color the pictures.

Learning patience and self-control is a great thing, but people with a bad temper hurt others and show bad choices.
Proverbs 14:29

Happy   Sad

Surprised   Angry

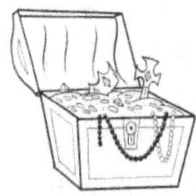

LESSON FIVE
A wise person stays calm even when he or she feels angry.
Proverbs 15:1

  **The Jewel in the Verse:** It is best to learn not to fly off the handle when you feel angry.

DISCUSSION AND ACTION: Look at the coloring picture for this verse. What do you think happened before this scene? How do you think the bigger bear feels in this picture? What could she do in this situation? What are her choices right now?

We may become angry about things that happen to us. Feeling angry is not bad or a sin. How you respond to your anger will show if you are acting wisely or not. How can the older bear act in a wise way? What would be a foolish or mean way to act?

Using felt and fabric (or if you prefer, paper), make a banner with the verse on it. Hang it in the house in a prominent place. It is a good reminder for everyone in the family. Remember that it is difficult for younger children to control their emotions, so begin a lesson that will last for years.

Teach your children to use words or "I statements" to tell of their anger, such as, "I feel angry because..." Teach them that talking about feelings is healthy. Over the years, teach your children to talk about the hurt, helplessness, shame, or sadness that underlies just about all angry feelings. In this way, they can get to the deeper issues, since anger is a secondary or protective feeling to help us avoid feeling something more painful. Many parents need to learn this, too. This week, look for others in our family who stay calm even when they feel angry. Tell them how wise they are acting.

Color the picture.

A wise person stays calm even when he or she feels angry.
Proverbs 15:1

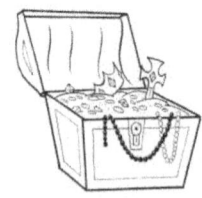

LESSON SIX

A gentle answer turns away anger, but more anger just stirs up more anger. A wise person will think about a way of responding to someone's angry words instead of blurting out their feelings.

Proverbs 15:1, 2

The Jewel in the Verse: Think before reacting to an emotional situation.

DISCUSSION AND ACTION: Have you ever heard kids in our family or at school say mean things to another child? How do you think that child feels? How do you think the mean child feels when he or she says bad things?

(Here, the parent may want to introduce the idea that people who act badly have learned to act that way, or at least they have been allowed to act that way. Many times, it is because they are hurting inside about something and they just want to hurt someone else).

The hurtful child may enjoy the power they feel when they hurt another person. This is useful for kids to realize so they can decide not to give the hurtful child the satisfaction of hurting them. If they understand that mean kids are often hurt inside, they may not take the words as personally and can enjoy a psychological buffer to the full weight of the aggression. This also gets kids thinking the psychological truth that there is an internal story in everyone. Bad behavior is usually not about something we did, it usually comes from somewhere inside the mean person. Telling children to ignore negative behavior is usually not effective by itself. If they can understand certain motives, they may be motivated to respond in an unexpected way.

Make up a story about the bunny. What might have happened at home to make him feel hurt and angry? What could the turtle be thinking right now? What are turtle's choices or options?

Color the picture.

A gentle answer turns away anger, but more anger just stirs up more anger. A wise person will think about a way of responding to someone's angry words instead of blurting out their feelings.
Proverbs 15:1,2

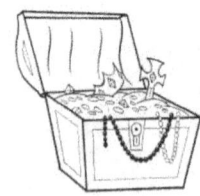

LESSON SEVEN
Trust in the Lord with all your heart.
Proverbs 3:5

The Jewel in the Verse: Trusting God is a journey. Learning to trust deeply is our destination.

DISCUSSION AND ACTION: What do you remember about our study on trust? Tell someone in the family what you know or remember about trust.

Repeat the "trust fall" activity if you want to do it again. This time, have another trustworthy person catch your child. Be sure they read and practice the earlier guidelines.

Ask adults to tell you a story that helped them learn about trusting God or trusting a godly person.

Look at the picture. What do you think grandma is saying to the young bear? Do you think grown-ups and older people could have some interesting stories? Wouldn't it be fun to tell a grandparent one of your stories, either something that happened or a made-up story from your imagination?

Call a grandparent, aunt, uncle, or friend and ask that person to tell you a story about trusting God.

See how many stories you can gather from your relatives about trusting God.

Trust in the Lord with all your heart.
Proverbs 3:5

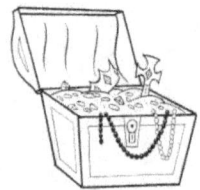

LESSON EIGHT

Telling something bad about one person to another person is wrong. That hurts people behind their backs. Friends you trust will not do that, but will keep things to themselves.

Proverbs 11:2

The Jewel in the Verse: Gossip is tempting, but it is very damaging. It is important to be true to your friends and acquaintances.

DISCUSSION AND ACTION: This lesson is about gossiping. The principal point is that we should not talk badly about someone when he or she isn't present. If you know something unpleasant or bad about someone, you should keep it to yourself. You may not understand everything that is really going on in that person's life. It is wrong to turn other people against someone or spread rumors that may not be true.

If someone was saying mean things about you behind your back, how do you think you would feel?

In this picture, bunny is telling bear some bad secrets about turtle. How does bear feel hearing bad things about someone else? Why would bunny say those things?
  (e.g., Bunny doesn't realize how hurtful it is, she is mad at turtle, wants bear to be mad at turtle so she can be closer to bunny.)

If the turtle found out what bad things bunny said, how would turtle feel? If turtle was mad at bunny, what should turtle do?
  (Friends could share how gossiping hurt their feelings and upset them. Talk about the problem!)

Color the picture.

Telling something bad about one person to another person is wrong. That hurts people behind their backs. Friends you can trust will not do that, but will keep things to themselves.
Proverbs 11:2

LESSON NINE
A wise person is careful and stays away from bad things.
Proverbs 14:15

The Jewel in the Verse: Wise people don't hang around trouble. They are smart enough to leave if things don't look good.

DISCUSSION AND ACTION: Look at the coloring picture for this verse. Make up a story telling what happened just before this picture. What is turtle thinking as he walks away? What were the turtle's other choices? Did he make the right choice?

Talk to your parents or grandparents about the ways they stay away from negative behaviors or bad situations. How do they help guide the family towards positive behaviors and good situations? How do they keep the family from getting off the track of what they should be doing? Look for these throughout your week.

Examples: Limiting certain activities, places, media; keeping a certain group of "good" friends; avoiding hanging out with people who are planning bad things; avoiding the bakery when you are very hungry; and avoiding turning on some shows that are scary or gross.

Color the picture.

A wise person is careful and stays away from bad things.
Proverbs 14:15

LESSON TEN
Trusting and obeying God starts you on a journey of learning wisdom and making good choices.
Proverbs 1: 7

  **The Jewel in the Verse:** Trusting God leads to good choices and good choices lead to a wise and happy life.

DISCUSSION AND ACTION: Every group of people (culture) in the world believes some things are right and some things are wrong. This is what we call moral values. Mom and Dad believe that God is our Creator (or Maker); that He loves us and He wants us to learn and practice good ways of behaving. Sometimes your mind tells you if something is good or bad. We call that your conscience.

What should you do if your mind starts to warn you about doing something? *(e.g., Child should stop and think, "Is there a rule about this behavior or not?" Also, the child can ask, "Will it hurt others?", "Would God think this is a good thing to do?" Child can also ask an older child or an adult for advice).*

FOR OLDER CHILDREN: Sometimes, the mind warns us that something is wrong when it is not really wrong. Sometimes, the mind forgets to warn us that something is wrong. How can we tell if something is right or wrong? Where do we go to find out what's right or wrong?
   (e.g., Bible, parents, rabbi, pastor, trusted friends)

Look at the picture. Turtle is trying to figure out what to do. What is he thinking? What do you think he should do? Some people might just walk by and say, "Somebody else will take care of it." Other people might think this is a God moment. God is giving them an opportunity to show kindness toward others - it is an opportunity they do not want to pass up.

Color the picture.

Trusting and obeying God starts you on a journey of learning wisdom and making good choices.
Proverbs 1:7

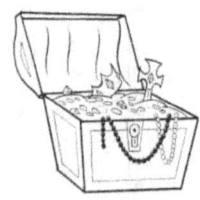

LESSON ELEVEN
A wise person learns the difference between right and wrong behavior and lives it.
Proverbs 16:21a

  **The Jewel in the Verse:** Learn what God thinks is good, and pattern your life around it.

DISCUSSION AND ACTION: *Read the story of the golden calf found in Exodus 32, Read 'n Grow Picture Bible, pp. 80-81or The Children's Bible, p. 67.*

Earlier, God told the Israelite people He didn't want them to worship man-made idols and statues, but they should only worship Him. Did Aaron and the people of Israel know that making the golden calf was wrong? Did they act as if they knew it was wrong? How can we tell the difference between right and wrong? How does it feel in your body when you know something is wrong? What might a person do if he or she knew something they were doing was wrong?

(e.g., He might hide or sneak around. She might cover up her behavior.)

Think of choices you make in your life every day. For example, you can choose whether to do your chores or not, or you can choose whether to argue with your sister or brother.

Would you know how to do the right thing in those situations? How do you know what is right, i.e. How could someone tell what is the right thing to do in as situation?

This discussion will help show your child that knowing what is right and doing the right thing are different challenges. It is one thing to know what is right or what is a good choice but it is another thing to actually make a good choice and act wisely. We must act on what we know and then we are able to show wise behavior.

Think about choices you made last week. Did your choices show wise behaviors? Was your behavior what you wanted others to see? Talk to the family about what you learned. What can we do when we haven't been wise?

(e.g., Learn from it, think of what we could have done differently, apologize to someone).

Let's look at the picture. What is happening? What are the characters thinking? What is pulling bunny in different directions? She is hungry and those are delicious looking carrots. How might this story end up? What could happen?

| Color the picture. |

A wise person learns the difference between right and wrong behavior and lives it.
Proverbs 16:21a

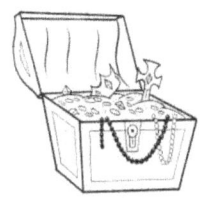

LESSON TWELVE
Sometimes getting away with something can feel fun. Sometimes a rule that says "no" makes us want to do it.
Proverbs 9:17

  **The Jewel in the Verse:** When you are told "no", sometimes it makes you want to disobey.

DISCUSSION AND ACTION: **Sometimes it can feel tempting to do something others tell you not to do. Have you ever seen a sign that reads, "Wet paint, don't touch"? Have you ever touched the object that is supposed to have wet paint on it? I have. Have you seen others do it? Sometimes when you're doing what you're told not to do and sneaking around, it can feel fun or exciting for a little while. Sometimes it can feel good to get away with something. Let's talk about what the words tempting or temptation mean. Being tempted means you have feelings that make you want something that would be wrong. We all have these temptations sometimes. You are not bad to want something that you shouldn't have or desire to do a behavior that would be wrong. That is temptation. What can a person do when he or she is feeling a temptation?**

(e.g., Stop, think about the rules, and think about the consequences. What would happen if you did the wrong thing and others were hurt by it or if they found out? Ask yourself if you would want someone else to do that thing to you.)

What would you feel like if someone did that to you?

Look at the picture. Turtle sees a pretty place to swim and it's a hot day. He's all ready to jump in and can almost feel how cool the water will be. What would turtle think if he felt tempted? What should he tell himself soon? Why?

| Color the picture. |

Sometimes getting away with something can feel fun.
Sometimes a rule that says "no" makes us want to do it.
Proverbs 9:17

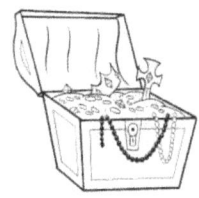
LESSON THIRTEEN
A wise person constantly learns from successes and failures; a righteous person adds to their learning.
Proverbs 9:9

  **The Jewel in the Verse:** Paying attention to your mistakes, or bad choices, is the only way to learn from them. Learning from mistakes means being strong enough to face them.

DISCUSSION AND ACTION: **Sometimes learning hurts. After we make mistakes or bad choices, we need the courage to look at what happened and admit it. Then we can learn to get better. People who don't take responsibility for what they do end up stunted like a little tree that never grows up. They do not learn from their mistakes and bad choices.**

Teach your child the three "make it right" statements when you wrong others: #1: "I was wrong," #2: "I will work on changing that behavior," and #3: I hope after you get through your hurt feelings, you can forgive me."

Secondary idea: We may feel sad about our mistakes or bad choices but we are not bad people just because we do something wrong. There is no room for feeling crushing shame or horrible embarrassment. If we do that, we will not look at our mistakes and learn from them because we will be too afraid of feeling ashamed of ourselves. Proper remorse allows us to feel badly for what we did to others while keeping our worth alive.

What were bear's choices after she spilled milk?
(e.g., Leave and pretend she didn't do it, stay and let it sit there, or stay and clean it up).

How does bear feel in the picture? How would she feel if she left without cleaning up? What should we do if we do something wrong when no one is watching? What should we do when we hurt another person?

Color the picture.

A wise person constantly learns from successes and failures; a righteous person adds to their learning.
Proverbs 9:9

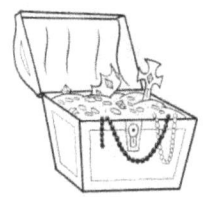

LESSON FOURTEEN

If you become cocky and think you know everything, you will end up falling on your face, but the humble person will grow in wisdom and his or her life will end up better.

Proverbs 11:17

The Jewel in the Verse: Avoid thinking you are better than others. Stay humble and you will grow.

DISCUSSION AND ACTION: This lesson is about being humble and not overly prideful or self-righteous. This is about thinking you are better than others, that you know everything, and bragging about it. Be humble and realize you do not know many things and that you may be weak in some areas. You have faults just like other people.

Have you ever thought you knew something but found out later it was wrong? I have. When you are so sure of something and it is not really true, it makes you think differently. After that, a person usually learns to tell themselves, "There are always other things I don't understand, things I might see the wrong way." When you think you know everything, learning stops. You probably don't know *everything*. Stay humble and realize there are other stories in people, about which you do not know.

In the picture, bear is thinking something. What do you imagine he is thinking? Why is bunny reading? What might she be thinking? What do you think will happen next?

| Color the picture. |

If you become cocky and think you know everything, you will end up falling on your face, but the humble person will grow in wisdom and his or her life will end up better.
Proverbs 11:17

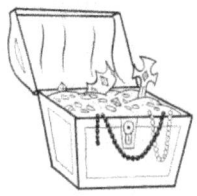

LESSON FIFTEEN

Unwise people don't care about learning from others; they just want to talk about their own opinions. Wise people love to learn more and more. They know that to answer before really listening to someone else is ridiculous.

Proverbs 18:2, 13

The Jewel in the Verse: Learn not to talk too much about your own opinions, but give other people time to talk and take them seriously. Be a good listener.

DISCUSSION AND ACTION: Do you like to learn new things? Do you think some people know about things that you don't? How would you learn from someone like that? Have you ever been around anyone who just likes to talk repeatedly about his or her opinion; someone who just likes to hear him/herself talk? It's boring, isn't it? Someone like that doesn't realize how much they could be learning if they listen to other people. Can you share one thing that you learned recently from someone else? Would you like to learn something new from someone this week and share it next time we get together?

What is baby bunny doing? Do you think children can learn from adults? Do you think adults can learn from children? Could children learn from each other? How will baby bunny feel when she learns something new?

Color the picture.

Unwise people don't care about learning from others; they just want to talk about their own opinions. Wise people love to learn about more and more things. They know that to answer before really listening to someone else is ridiculous.
Proverbs 18:2, 13

LESSON SIXEEN
A wise person admits his or her wrong behavior and works to change it.
Proverbs 28:13

The Jewel in the Verse: When you hurt someone, don't be defensive - admit what you did and start changing it.

DISCUSSION AND ACTION: Sometimes, people do things that hurt others. Usually we just say, "I'm sorry," and go on with our lives. There is another way to ask for forgiveness that is helpful for children and parents alike. It has four parts:

#1 - Tell the person what you did wrong. Admit that you have hurt them and tell the specific behavior that you did (say the behavior and the feeling). For example, "I'm sorry that I yelled at you. I know that hurt you."

#2 - Tell the person that you should not have hurt him or her. Explain that you will work to change that behavior. For example, "I should not have hurt you. I will change how I handle my anger so I don't yell."

#3 - Ask the person to forgive you for your words or behavior. Give the person time to do this. For example, "I hope you can forgive me when you are ready."

#4 - Offer to do something that shows you are sorry. For example, "I will do your chores for 2 days."

Let us pretend that you called your sister or brother an unkind name. If you want to respond wisely, you might say:
#1 - "I know I hurt you when I called you that name."

#2 - "I should not have hurt you. I will work to control myself and not call you a name again."
#3 - "Will you forgive me for calling you that name?"
#4 - "I will let you borrow my toys whenever you want them this week." Your sibling knows that you understand his or her feelings and care about him or her, so you will work to stop this behavior in the future.

Practice this way of making things right and asking for forgiveness with people in your life.

Parents, be sure to model the four steps when you are wrong.

Look at the coloring picture for this verse. Make up a story about the picture. How did the toy get broken? How did the girl bear feel when she broke it? What did she do after she broke it? What might the bear say to the bunny? How might the bunny feel? What might the bunny say?

| Color the picture. |

A wise person admits his or her wrong behavior and works to change it.
Proverbs 28:13

LESSON SEVENTEEN
Do not act like mean and violent bullies. The way they live is not a good way for you to live.
Proverbs 3:31

The Jewel in the Verse: Avoid using anger and bullying to control others. That's an ugly way to live.

DISCUSSION AND ACTION: **Why do you think people act in a mean way?**
(e.g. People may be mean to others, but those people may not feel like they can respond to the bully, so the person might find another person to pick on. People may think others don't like them and act badly as a result. People might act in a mean way if their parents have allowed them to hurt others (and get away with it) without really being sorry.)

Why is anger such a hard feeling to control?
(e.g., Because among all the feelings, anger often makes us feel like we want to hurt someone.)

What can a wise person do when he or she is feeling really angry?
(e.g., Stop, think, and say your feelings. Tell yourself you're okay even though you are upset. Walk away. Count to 10. Take some deep breaths. Remember, the other person might be hurting inside and may not know what to do with his or her feelings; ask the person if he or she wants to talk about it instead of hurting you.)

In the picture, what are the bullies doing? How do the bullies want turtle and the bear in the wheelchair to feel? What might the turtle and bear think while the bullies are laughing at them?

> Color the picture.

Do not act like mean and violent bullies. The way they live is not a good way for you to live.
Proverbs 3:31

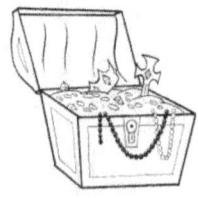
LESSON EIGHTEEN
Wise and strong people can control their tempers.

Proverbs 14:29

The Jewel in the Verse: You are smart and powerful when you learn to control your anger.

DISCUSSION AND ACTION: What does it mean to "control your temper"? Can you think of a time when you were not able to control your temper? What did you do? What happened to make you so angry that you lost control or did something hurtful?

Let's pretend you and a sibling are playing a game. You roll the dice and land on the square that makes you lose the game. Your sibling starts to laugh. Show what a foolish response and a wise response would look like.

(e.g., An unwise response would be a negative or aggressive reaction; a wise response would be saying, "It bothers me when you make fun of me losing. I feel hurt (or angry). I won't play with you if you do that again.")

Talk to family members about their tempers. How do they control their anger when they feel it? List some ways a person can control his or her anger.

(e.g. Counting to 10, walking away, taking deep breaths, think that the other person that must be hurting, reminding yourself, "I'm okay even though I am mad," or expressing feelings in words without hurting others.)

Hang the list in a noticeable place. Keep adding to the list as you identify new, wise ways of handling anger. What are some signs that you might not be handling your anger in a wise manner?

Why is turtle angry? What are her choices? What is she doing, and what is she thinking while she is angry?

| Color the picture. |

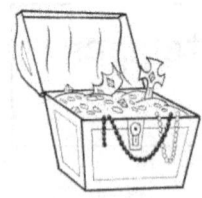
LESSON NINETEEN
The wise heart will receive instruction.
Proverbs 10:8

  **The Jewel in the Verse:** Desire to correct your mistakes with everything in you.

DISCUSSION AND ACTION: For children, instruction or teaching usually come from parents or teachers. Sometimes, learning from them feels good and is easy, but sometimes it is hard to learn from certain people. It might seem easier to become bored or even to argue with that person.

Here is a way to help you learn how to be wise. Next time you are doing something that is unwise, your parents may ask you three questions:
1. What are you doing?
2. What are you supposed to be doing?
3. What are you going to do now?

This will help you look at your choices so you have a chance to make good ones.

> Parents: The point to this series of questions is to have your child internalize a process of reflection, consciously "diagnosing" the problem, and identifying the decisions available.

The three questions will help you stop, focus on your behavior, and give you a chance to make a better choice. If you still decide to act unwisely, you may receive a consequence for your actions. So, when you hear the questions, stop, think, and answer honestly.

Practice using the three-question technique now in a role-play. Act out a situation. Ask then answer the three questions. Reversing roles is often fun for children, and for us! For example, a child is arguing with her parent about doing her homework.

Parent asks,
1. **"Honey, what are you doing?"** (Answer for them if they don't answer correctly: "I am arguing with mom.")
2. **"Now, what should you be doing?"** (Answer: I should be doing my homework instead of playing my game and arguing.")
3. **"What are you going to choose?"** ("I should choose to stop arguing and do my homework." If the child is not making a good choice to stop, tell her that continued arguing is a bad choice that will lead to a consequence. Maybe she will have to fold laundry or do one of your chores for taking up your time with arguing.)

Parents should pray that a few of these situations happen this week so you can try out your three questions. Watch how it curtails arguing.

Tell your child: **"When you hear the questions, you will get the chance to answer them. Try to remember the verse and learn from the situation. Good luck on figuring out your choices."**

Look at the picture. What is the bear trying to do and why? What is the bear thinking? Is she being pulled in different directions inside her mind? What do you think she wants to do? What do you think the bear should do?

Color the picture.

The wise heart will receive instruction.
Proverbs 10:8

LESSON TWENTY
A wise person has other wise people for friends.
Proverbs 13:20

The Jewel in the Verse: One of the smartest things you can do is hang out with wise and kind people.

DISCUSSION AND ACTION: *Parent chooses a child (or asks for a volunteer)*

Let's pretend you and a friend are playing with toys at school, aftercare, or church. You find a small toy that you really like, and you want to take it home with you. You can put it in your pocket and the teacher will not know you have taken it. You tell your friend that you want to take the toy. Let's show how a wise friend would help you in this situation. What would a wise friend say or do? What might a foolish friend say or do?"

Later, ask if a child can identify something similar in their lives and role-play again. Show how friends can influence in positive or negative ways.

I would like you to talk to members of our family about their friends. Find out what they have learned about choosing wise friends. How do they know if a friend is wise? Have they ever had a foolish friend? Did they stay friends? Did your family member help that person? Maybe your family member can even remember a time when he or she was not a wise friend to someone.

What is happening in the picture? How do you think the friends feel? Why do you think they feel that way? Do you think the friends are wise or foolish? How can you tell? Do you have wise and kind friends? What do you like to do together?

Let's try to spend time with a wise or kind friend this week.

Color the picture.

A wise person has other wise people for friends.
Proverbs 13:20

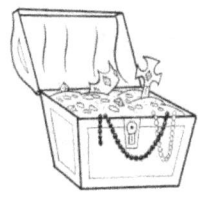

LESSON TWENTY-ONE
You can teach wise people because they will happily listen to you and consider your advice. Don't waste your time trying to teach foolish people who refuse to listen or get mad at you for your helpful words.
Proverbs 9:8

  **The Jewel in the Verse:** Expect wise people to learn from others but if someone doesn't listen, avoid them.

Trying to teach someone who is not teachable (someone who doesn't want to listen) will not be effective, no matter how true your words are, or how much they need to hear it. Do not continually try to get someone to understand you if he or she is not listening. Choose someone who is teachable, someone who will listen, or someone who will try to understand you.

DISCUSSION AND ACTION: **Have you ever heard two people having an argument? Usually in an argument, each person wants a chance to speak. Some arguers do not listen to the other person. What are some ways you could avoid getting into arguments?**

(e.g., Be sure to listen to the other person first. Talk about your feelings in a calm and kind way. Repeat what you heard the person say to show you really did hear it. Tell the person you don't want to argue. Take turns sharing your feelings with each other. Work to identify a solution that will suit both of you. Many adults do not often act wisely in arguments. We would do well to help our children learn to look for these situations and know how to communicate effectively to minimize arguments. We should practice it ourselves.)

In the next picture, what is happening? What is the bunny feeling? What is the bear feeling? What do you think the bunny should do?

Color the picture.

You can teach wise people because they will happily listen to you and consider your advice. Don't waste your time trying to teach foolish people who refuse to listen or get mad at you for your helpful words.
Proverbs 9:8

LESSON TWENTY-TWO
A wise person obeys the teaching of the Lord.
Proverbs 28:7

The Jewel in the Verse: After you learn what God says is good, be sure to put it into action (obey Him).

DISCUSSION AND ACTION: **Let's talk about ways our family tries to obey God's teachings. Do you think every family looks for ways to follow God? Why or why not? Some families may not think about following and obeying God. Ask your parents or grandparents to tell you about some things they have done to try to follow God more. How have they changed their beliefs and behaviors about following God?**

Look at the coloring picture. How is this family obeying the Lord? They are showing several ways to obey the Lord in this one picture. Can you find three?

(Suggested answers: The parent is showing kindness to the child on her back. The family is being friendly to friends. The family is going to a meeting of other people of faith.)

Color the picture.

A wise person obeys the teaching of the Lord.
Proverbs 28:7

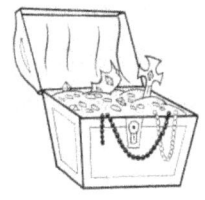
LESSON TWENTY-THREE

Trust God with all your heart and don't think you know better than He does. In all your ways, follow Him and He will help you be successful. Do not be unteachable, but fear the Lord and avoid bad things.
Proverbs 3:5-7

  **The Jewel in the Verse:** God made you, so He knows best - there must be some things He knows that you don't know. If you find yourself questioning God, trust what He says.

Learning to follow God's ways and avoid going against them is the theme here. If you think you know everything and believe you are always right, it will lead to trouble. Trust God and do good things while avoiding wrong things.

DISCUSSION AND ACTION: Have you ever said to yourself about one of our family rules, "That's a dumb rule. I think it is okay to do whatever I want to do, even if they think I shouldn't do it. There's nothing wrong with it." Yes, we all have thought that from time to time and if you haven't, you will in the future. Most rules have a good reason even if you can't see the reason right now. How does it feel to trust mom and dad about rules that don't seem to make sense to you? Is it easy or hard? Can you share one rule that doesn't seem to be necessary? Don't worry, you won't be in trouble. Is it hard to trust God when He tells us some things are good to do and some things are bad to do, especially when you don't see why?

(Here the parents may wish to share a rule they thought was dumb growing up, especially if the child cannot come up with one themselves.)

What did bear think when his parents told him not to eat more cookies before bedtime? Why would his parents make up that rule? What is bear thinking?

Color the picture.

Trust God with all your heart and don't think you know better than He does. In all your ways, follow Him and He will help you be successful. Do not be unteachable, but fear the Lord and avoid bad things.
Proverbs 3:5-7

LESSON TWENTY-FOUR

Remember or memorize what God says and remind yourself as you go through each day. Remember what your mother and father teach you; keep them close to you, as if they are like a necklace around your neck or your favorite T-shirt wrapped around you. They will guide you toward good choices and when you memorize them, they will speak to you in your mind. Taking instruction and learning from mistakes are a part of a good life. Wise teachings will be like a lamp or a light for you.

Proverbs 6:20-23

  **The Jewel in the Verse:** Learn truth and place it deep within your mind and heart so it will guide you when you're not sure what to do.

Okay, this one is a bit long. You might take a few days with it. DISCUSSION AND ACTION: **What does a lamp or a light do? Imagine you had to get across a dark room that you had never been in before. You would probably go slowly and bump into things. You might bang your knee or bump your head. Hopefully, you would learn how to go around things or how to duck your head, but only after you bumped into them. Now, imagine you had a flashlight. How would this be better as you go across the dark room? Would you make as many mistakes or get as many bruises that way? God's teachings are like a flashlight for us. Living by God's "flashlight" will light up our path and keep us from getting hurt. If God's teachings are like the light, how does the bear feel on the lighted path? Do you think he feels comfortable, safe, or relaxed? Why? How can the light help him? What if he chose the dark path and did not have a light? How might he feel on the dark path? Can the dark be scary sometimes? Why?**

Color the picture.

Remember or memorize what God says and remind yourself as you go through each day. Remember what your mother and father teach you; keep them close to you, as if they are like a necklace around your neck or your favorite T-shirt wrapped around you. They will guide you into good choices and when you memorize them, they will speak to you in your mind. Taking instruction and learning from mistakes are a part of a good life. Wise teachings will be like a lamp or a light for you."
Proverbs 6:20 - 23

LESSON TWENTY-FIVE
The Lord gives wisdom.
Proverbs 2:6

The Jewel in the Verse: Everything centers on God. He is our Creator.

Review from where true wisdom comes.
DISCUSSION AND ACTION: **Do you remember the story of Solomon? How did he get wisdom?**

(e.g., He asked God for it because he knew it was important.)

Tell the story again to a family member or friend. Ask that person to pray for you to be wise as you continue this study.

Look at the coloring picture. Pick one of the children in the picture and imagine some details about the character. What does that character like to do for fun? Which games does he or she like to play? What do you think that character likes or dislikes about school?

All people can learn about wisdom. Nobody knows all about it yet. Sometimes, people make foolish choices. What have we learned about wise and unwise choices? Even foolish choices can help us learn for the future.

Note to Parent: It's important that we do not expect children to be perfect in their choices. In fact, childhood is a series of mistakes and poor choices as children learn wise choices, rather than a string of successes with an occasional flop. Get this straight and your parenting will be easier and better, for you and your children.

It is important that children learn to feel regret, guilt, and sadness about poor choices, but children should not feel ashamed (or bad about the self). Shame creates a natural inclination to avoid uncomfortable situations, which can interfere with a person's ability to learn from unwise choices. Handling poor choices means we are willing to correct damage if we can.

Color the picture.

The Lord gives wisdom.
Proverbs 2:6

Review all the verses. Read Proverbs 2:1-12.

Activity: Make a poster that shows a fork in the road (to represent decisions to make). Label one path, "The way of the wise" and the other path, "The way of the unwise." Children can draw things on each path. The foolish path may have negative or scary things as a bridge that is out, danger signs, snake in the grass, vulture on a carcass, etc. Try to get the child to use their imagination without prompting too much. Use their images or ones they cut out from magazines. The wise path may have positive images, such as apple trees, money, gold, friends, cookies, or whatever represents good and success to your little one. For young children, the images should be very concrete, like a hamburger or ice cream. For older children, consider including images of cigarettes, drugs, fighting, stealing, reckless behavior, etc.

Use the poster to facilitate a discussion about the choices we made last week and the ones we made today. Be prepared to model answers to get the ball rolling.

Possible questions:
Which road do you want to take in your life?
There are many forks in our road of life. How can we choose the right road at each fork? Where does the foolish path lead? Where does the wise path lead?

It might be hard to tell the difference between the wise and unwise paths. You might think one path looks good, but it might not be. Trust in your parents and God to guide you onto the right path. Younger children who still think in either/or terms may have problems with this but older children will start to grasp it. Leave the poster up for a few weeks and refer back to it as needed.

Right and Wrong, Morality, and Sin

The three, near-Eastern, monotheistic faiths (joined by the notion that God is one and He is personal) are Judaism, Christianity, and Islam. They form the belief that life is lived within a moral context. This moral standard is in the very nature of God and God determines what is good or bad in the moral sphere. We get these teachings of right or wrong through "natural law" (natural revelation, law "written on our hearts") and more specifically, through the revelation of a Holy Scripture. Furthermore, prophets or teachers within each faith have expounded upon the moral laws of life expressed in these scriptures. Since the destruction of the Jewish Temple in 70 A.D., Judaism's rabbinical leaders have further explained a biblical morality and a biblical way of life. Christians believe that Jesus came "not to destroy the law, but to fulfill it," and that in Him, is the embodiment of God and moral truth. Islam maintains that Mohammed and the revelation of the Koran are the final arbiters regarding who God is and what he expects morally.

You may or may not come from any of these monotheistic faiths and may have other sources that determine your moral standards. If you have used this book, you likely see value in this particular book of Proverbs, which is part of the "wisdom literature," and the Jewish Scriptures used in this study (or the Old Testament).

I purposely limited the study to the "Old Testament" because all three monotheistic faiths value this content. In each of these faiths, breaking the moral law is sin. These faiths also teach that a fact of being human is that we break some of these moral laws from time to time, both internally (in our hearts/will) and externally, through behavior.

For the modern secular mind, the concept of sin is often remote or nonexistent. A famous psychiatrist, Dr. Karl Menninger, even wrote a book many years ago called, *What Ever Happened to Sin?* For many people, it has disappeared. In an increasingly secular world where absolute standards outside of the self (eternal moral truths) have no anchor point, morality is in the eye of the beholder. What is right and wrong takes on a much less imperative and accountable meaning.

No longer tied to violating our Creator's perfect goodness, doing something "wrong" means answering to no one - unless you are caught. Since morality not anchored is a drifting, changing morality, any transgression is akin to a traffic violation in a particular country. You may get a ticket because the people do not like what you did, but you pay the fine and travel to another country where the rules are slightly different. Traffic laws (and the violation of them) have no strong sense of accountability or compulsion.

The modern sense of right and wrong appears to be increasingly watered down with pragmatism (what works) or narcissism (what's good for only me). If an individual's life is like a ship, these changes in morality have the effect of dropping the compass and map overboard. Navigating life becomes either doing what works (going wherever the wind blows) or what feels good to the captain ("Over there are clouds, and over there it looks sunny. Let's go where it's sunny. I've always liked the beach."). With the proliferation of pragmatism and narcissism as a basis for values, the prospects of reaching the destination of a well-lived, morally-guided life are shrinking.

We certainly cannot expect a drifting culture to support us in this journey. This trend is the primary reason I wanted to study the process of decision-making and choosing wisely with my children. It is arguably the most important skill in life.

A Suggestion of How to Teach Children about Sin

An entomological study of "sin" in the Bible reveals a word that comes from archery. The purpose of archery is to hit the target, and not just any place on the target, but the bull's-eye. The word for sin is the word used when missing the bull's-eye or missing that at which you are aiming.

Perhaps you can illustrate this with your child with rolled up socks and a trashcan (or anything that you can safely throw into a container). Our goal is to throw the socks, one at a time, into the can. If the socks go in the can, we have achieved success. Achieving moral success is like trying to do what God teaches us to do. We hit the bucket and the socks go in – we have achieved our goal. Sometimes (be sure you demonstrate this visually) we don't hit the bucket. We might feel sad and disappointed, and we want to become more successful at hitting the bucket. Similarly, when we make a bad choice in life, it is like throwing a bad shot that misses the bucket. We have missed our target. We can ask God to help us grow so that we can be more successful at achieving our goal and His goodness.

Through the Bible

Using all they have learned about wisdom, you can now take your child through the Bible stories. Leave the treasure chest picture with memory verses up in your home, for a reference. You can help improve retention by "spaced learning," where you review content a few days or weeks apart, to help anchor the information.

Many of the lessons may seem very similar; however, they each have a special message or a special burst of wisdom. This subtle repetition of concepts will help your child learn about wisdom in different ways. Your child will begin to make important connections between words, pictures, stories, and real-world experiences. Encourage your child to activate prior knowledge (e.g., What did we learn about wisdom last week? What foolish or wise choice did you make this week?). Build on that knowledge with new stories, new proverbs, new examples, and new experiences.

You can use the following Bible Chart for this study. You may photocopy it if you need additional sheets. Glue them to the inside of a file folder or a homemade book to keep them safe and unwrinkled throughout this part of the study.

Each lesson includes the following steps:
1. Read a Bible story from your book.
2. Ask these questions about the story:
    What can we learn about God from this story?
    Who is wise in this story? Why?
    Who is unwise or foolish in the story? Why?
3. Record your answers on the chart.

Example: Story Name - David & Goliath
What did you learn about God?
(God prepares His people for their work. God protects His people.)
Who is wise? (David)
Why? (David did what he believed God wanted him to do and he trusted God in the face of danger. He trusted God even more than himself.)
Who is unwise? (Saul, Goliath, Philistines)
Why? (Saul was too scared to trust God; Goliath and the Philistines opposed God and rejected His wisdom.) Your answers may vary from this example. On a regular basis, review what you have written on the chart. In this study, you will find that the same person can be wise in one story and foolish in another. Use this fact to explain that our lives are full of choices and sometimes we choose foolishly. A wise person who fails will repent (or turn away) from any behavior that "misses the mark" (sin), learn from their mistakes, and grow in wisdom as a result.

From the chart, you will also build up a list of attributes of God, derived inductively from your reading.

You may read one story a day or three a week.

May this time be one of growth for you and your children, as you learn about God and His ways.

BIBLE CHART

Story Name	What can we learn about God in this story?	Who is wise in this story?	What wise behaviors do we see?	Who is foolish in this story?	What foolish behaviors do we see?

Owl Cards: Please photocopy as needed. Allow children to color the owls if they choose to.

Stick Puppets: Please photocopy as needed. Color then cut out the characters.

Stick Puppets: Please photocopy as needed. Color then cut out the characters.

Stick Puppets: Please photocopy as needed. Color then cut out the characters.

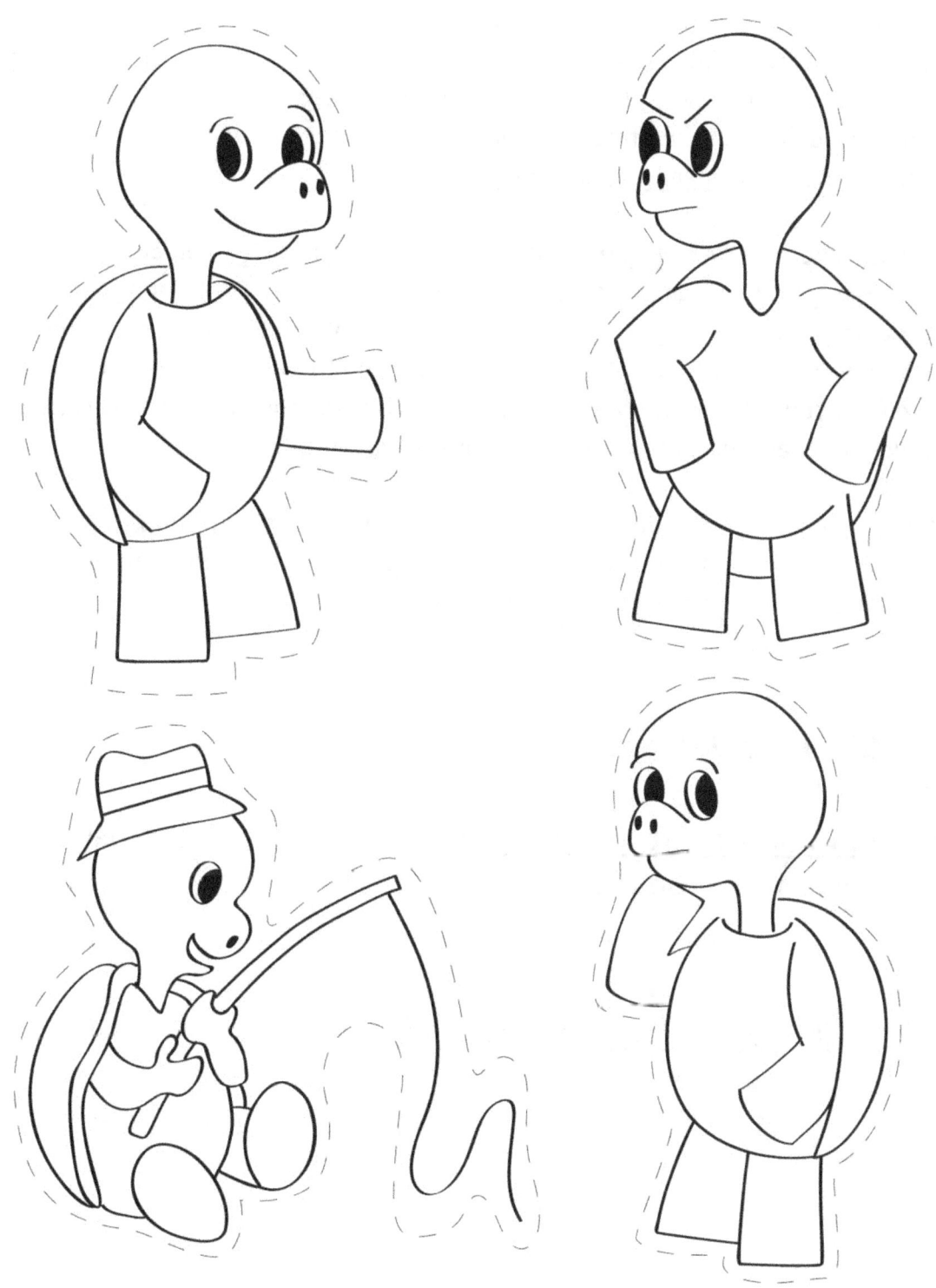

About the Author

Dale Simpson, PhD, has fathered and home schooled five children. As a practicing psychologist for more than 36 years, he has counseled children, teens, adults and couples and currently practices in Venice, Florida. Dr. Simpson is a cofounder and former publisher of **Homeschooling Today Magazine**, wrote Inside the Family column for the magazine, served as a featured speaker at numerous parenting and homeschooling conferences, and is the publisher of Learning for Life Press. At Learning for Life Press, visitors can download free resources to help them in their family's journey. www.learningforlifepress.com

Dr. Simpson has written Homeschooling for Life, A Study in Wisdom, the Think It, Feel It, Say It! board game and he publishes The Easy to Make Paper Airplane Book. Homeschooling for Life gives parents practical solutions for emotional and spiritual growth during the homeschooling years. **Each chapter has discussion questions to further the learning process. This unique book has both a father's and psychologist's perspective** with a distinctively Christian world view.

The engaging game Think It, Feel It, Say It!, combines lots of fun with self-expression, identifying feelings, thinking through difficult encounters, and gaining self-confidence. It is for ages 6 and up.

Special FREE Resources

Stop by www.learningforlifepress.com for free resources, newsletter, and recommended products.

Email: info@learningforlifepress.com

Other family resources available through Learning for Life Press

The Easy to Make Paper Airplane Book by Lane Simpson
Your children's fun will take off while they learn the basics of flight from this easy-to-use book. All designs have step-by-step instructions tested by children worldwide. All your children need is notebook paper and off they go!

Web site: www.learningforlifepress.com
Get your copy today at Amazon
ISBN 978-0-9988624-0-8

Homeschooling for Life, 2nd edition

Wouldn't you like to have access to an experienced homeschooling psychologist without having to make an appointment? Well, your ship has come in. Homeschooling for Life gives the practical, stress reducing help you need. Rather than a book about teaching classes, this unique book blends professional and personal experience with Dr. Simpson's down to earth approach to the home school lifestyle. Follow these important emotional and spiritual tools for a solid foundation and a successful home school experience.

Dale Simpson, PhD, has fathered and home school 5 children. A practicing psychologist for more than 37 years, he has counseled children, teens, adults, and couples and currently practices in Venice, Florida. Dr. Simpson was a cofounder and publisher of Homeschooling Today Magazine, wrote a column Inside the Family for the magazine, and served as a featured speaker at numerous home school conferences. Visit us at www.learningforlifepress.com for more products and free resources.

Think It, Feel It, Say It! Board Game

Do you want your family to learn about others, communicate better, and practice making wise choices while having tons of fun? The Think It, Feel It, Say It! game is just what you need. Enjoy the discussions, the laughs, and the wonderful interactions. Your children and your family will grow together!

The colorful and engaging game combines fun with self-expression, identifying feelings, thinking through difficult encounters, learning wisdom, and gaining self-confidence. Parents and children will deepen their knowledge of each other and make fun memories at the same time.

Ages: 6 – Above
Players: 2 – 8

The Think It, Feel It, Say It! Board Game is available for purchase through www.learningforlifepress.com

Visit us for our free newsletter, downloads and resources.
Email: info@learningforlifepress.com

A Study in Wisdom, 2nd edition
ISBN 978-0-9988624-5-3